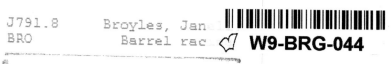

Barrel Racing

Janell Broyles

rosen
central ™

The Rosen Publishing Group, Inc., New York

Published in 2006 by The Rosen Publishing Group, Inc.
29 East 21st Street, New York, NY 10010

Library of Congress Cataloging-in-Publication Data

Broyles, Janell.
Barrel racing/Janell Broyles.—1st ed.
        p. cm.—(The world of rodeo)
Includes bibliographical references and index.
ISBN 1-4042-0543-8 (library binding)
1. Barrel racing—Juvenile literature. I. Title. II. Series.
GV1834.45.B35B76 2006
791.8'4—dc22

                                                                    2005017542

Manufactured in Malaysia

On the cover: A barrel racer competes in the annual White Mountain Apache Tribal Fair and Rodeo, held in Whiteriver, Arizona.

Contents

Introduction

Barrel racing is one of the few rodeo events in which animals and humans work cooperatively to defeat a common foe—in this case, the clock. Rather than wrestling, riding, bucking, throwing, or trampling each other into submission, horse and rider are united in a common purpose—to complete a cloverleaf pattern among three barrels as quickly as possible.

Entering the arena at full gallop, the horse and rider round each of the three barrels without knocking them over. A five-second penalty is imposed if a barrel is knocked over. Having weaved through the course, the horse and rider then exit the arena, still galloping at full speed. A winning time in barrel racing varies between about thirteen to twenty-two seconds, depending on the size of the arena. Achieving a winning time takes enormous skill and a unique sympathy between human and beast.

Barrel racing is a million-dollar sport on today's professional rodeo circuits. Thousands of riders participate at all levels—county fairs, small-town rodeos, charity events, as well as the better-known big-time rodeos. Barrel racing requires a horse that is fast, tough, and graceful, and a rider who knows how to get the most out of every turn and every sprint.

A barrel racer and her horse streak past a barrel at a rodeo held in Pinedale, Wyoming. Every year in July, Pinedale hosts the Green River Rendezvous, a celebration of the area's history and its Mountain Man heritage. The Rendezvous Rodeo is one of the most popular events of the festival. Wyoming, known as the Cowboy State, is home to some of North America's oldest and most important rodeos, including Cheyenne Frontier Days, the Cody Stampede, and the Sheridan Rodeo. Smaller local rodeos are also popular and are usually held on Sundays.

THE BIRTH OF BARREL RACING

CHAPTER 1

The origins of any one particular rodeo event can be hard to pin down. Undoubtedly, the men and women who handled livestock (such as horses, cattle, and sheep) had always engaged in informal contests with each other to determine who was the fastest at catching or subduing an animal. What we call professional rodeo grew out of just such casual ranch pastimes, as cowhands in the American West would take turns trying to stay on top of a wild horse or an even wilder bull. Ironically, it wasn't until the cowboy way of life began to die out in the late nineteenth century that these spontaneous games started to evolve into a spectator sport that offered substantial prize money to the winners of each event.

BARREL RACING AND RODEO

Barrel racing's origins, unlike cattle roping or cutting, are not directly traced to ranch work. Instead, the event evolved from the timed relay races that were added to traveling Wild West shows.

Wild West show entrepreneurs may have gotten the idea for events such as barrel racing from an older equestrian tradition called gymkhana. Gymkhana evolved from military cavalry training, in which riders demonstrated their skills on horseback while performing various tasks—such as weaving through poles, picking up pegs, or racing around and jumping over obstacles. These exercises were designed to sharpen the riders' horsemanship skills in preparation for battle. But while it began as an exhibition sport, the combination of explosively fast horses and superb riding that barrel racing requires has made its popularity grow until it is now considered one of the most popular competitive rodeo sports among spectators, second only to bull riding.

WOMEN IN THE RODEO

An important reason for barrel racing's popularity is the fact that it is open to female participation. Before rodeo became highly organized and regulated, many women participated—and excelled—in bull riding and other events, but women-only events were eventually dropped from most programs due to the dangerousness of the rodeo sports.

The turn of the twentieth century was a sort of golden age for women in rodeo. As Mary Lou LeCompte highlights in her book, *Cowgirls of the Rodeo*, from the late 1890s through the 1920s, cowgirls participated in North America's most important rodeo competitions, like the Calgary Stampede (in Calgary, Alberta, Canada), the Pendleton Round-Up (in Pendleton, Oregon), and the World Series Rodeo in New York City's Madison Square Garden.

Women who had been raised on ranches often worked with their fathers and brothers on such chores as shoeing horses and herding and roping cattle (in order to pasture, dehorn, castrate, brand, or medicate them, or load them onto trucks bound for market). As a result, these female ranchers were often every bit as

William F. "Buffalo Bill" Cody staged outdoor Western-themed plays, featuring hundreds of cast members. Buffalo Bill's Wild West shows (as advertised in the poster above) introduced the public to the riding and roping events that would form the core of modern rodeo.

Wild West Shows, Fiestas, and Cowboy Tournaments

Most historians credit Buffalo Bill Cody with creating the modern rodeo. His Wild West shows drew thousands of spectators in North America and Europe. They were awed by trick riding, sharpshooting, and simulated Indian attacks. Cody's success proved that crowds would pay to see exciting displays of cowboy skills. As a result, rodeos began to spring up in towns all across the United States and Canada.

skilled at horsemanship and livestock management as cowboys were. The cowgirls were respected for their riding and roping skills in rodeo contests, in which they competed as equals with their male counterparts and were major draws. Some, including Dorothy Morrell and Tad Lucas, even became rodeo stars.

In the 1930s, this all began to change. Some rodeo events began to be organized under the Rodeo Association of America, a group of rodeo managers and promoters who sanctioned events, selected judges, and established purses and point systems to determine all-around champions. Many of these managers and promoters were uncomfortable with the idea of women as serious competitors in rodeo and instead employed attractive "Ranch Girls" as paid performers in exhibition riding events. Cowgirls soon found fewer opportunities to compete in legitimate rodeo.

A few cowgirls managed to continue to compete in rodeo. However, when one of the last great cowgirl bronc riders of the era, Bonnie McCarroll of Idaho, was thrown and trampled at the Pendleton Round-Up in 1929, her death served effectively to end female participation in rodeo for decades. In the wake of McCarroll's death, cowgirl bronc riding was dropped from the Pendleton Round-Up, and soon thereafter from most other rodeos. Cowgirls' participation in professional rodeo was virtually nonexistent by the end of World War II (1939–1945).

Bonnie McCarroll is thrown from a horse named Silver in this undated photograph. She emerged unhurt from this fall, but McCarroll would be killed during a saddle bronc event at the 1929 Pendleton Round-Up in Oregon. While being thrown from the wild horse, her foot got caught in a stirrup, and she was dragged to her death.

The tide began to turn in favor of renewed female participation in rodeo in 1948, with the founding of the Girls Rodeo Association (GRA). This group successfully pushed for rodeo committees and producers to hold all-women rodeos, with barrel racing being the most commonly produced event. The GRA evolved into the Women's Professional Rodeo Association (WPRA), which today has more than 2,000 members and sanctions 800 barrel races a year in conjunction with the rodeos of the Professional Rodeo Cowboys Association (PRCA). The WPRA's sister organization, the Professional Women's Rodeo Association (PWRA), sanctions all-women rodeos across the United States and holds an annual world championship. The events include bareback and bull riding and calf roping.

BARREL-RACING CHAMPIONS

Barrel racing has been slow to organize at a championship level, since it began as an exhibition entertainment, rather than a competitive sport. It wasn't until 1959, when the first National Finals Rodeo (NFR) was held, that rules became more standardized and purses began to grow in value. But that didn't keep some truly extraordinary women from making their names as barrel-racing champions. As the event continues to grow in popularity, these athletes' careers will serve as enduring benchmarks for excellence in the sport.

ELENOR "SISSY" THURMAN

Sissy Thurman's career spanned the era when barrel racing evolved from the 1940s-era paid performances of "Ranch Girl"-type riders to a truly competitive rodeo event. She used her competitive barrel-racing experience to become director of the GRA, creating more—and more varied—opportunities for professional rodeo competition for all the women who came after her.

Born in 1934 in Galveston, Texas, Thurman began riding horses when she was only five years old and competed in her first barrel race at age eleven. At the beginning of her career, she served as a rodeo queen for local rodeos and stock shows. She was also a tap dancer and a teacher before she began professionally riding in rodeos. Thurman became one of the country's top barrel racers, at one point setting the fastest time in NFR barrel racing.

National Cowgirl Hall of Fame barrel racer Elenor "Sissy" Thurman appears above in competition. After her racing career ended, she served as barrel-racing director of the Girls Rodeo Association (GRA), formed in 1948, one year after the first-ever all-girl rodeo was held in Amarillo, Texas. This rodeo drew participants from New Mexico, Oklahoma, Texas, and Missouri.

After becoming the barrel-racing director for the GRA, Thurman held clinics that taught other women the finer points of barrel racing. She was killed in an automobile accident in 1968, on her way to a rodeo in Waco, Texas. Thurman was inducted into the Cowgirl Hall of Fame in 1975.

MARTHA JOSEY

After many years of barrel racing without attracting much attention, Martha Josey exploded into prominence in 1964, on her horse Cebe Reed. That year, the pair won fifty-two barrel races in a row. Josey qualified for her first National Finals Rodeo in 1968, and she qualified again in 1969. Later, on her horse Sonny Bit

Rodeo

The word "rodeo" comes from the Spanish word *rodear*, meaning "to surround or gather together" a herd of cattle or other livestock. It was at such ranch roundups that cowboys would show off their riding and roping skills, and the word "rodeo" evolved into a term for generally informal and spontaneous contests of ranch skills. During the great cattle drives of the nineteenth and twentieth centuries, cowboys from many different ranches would come together in one place to test and show off their skills and place bets on the competitors. It wasn't until later that these informal gatherings became organized and outside spectators were charged admission.

O'Both, she went to the NFR four years in a row, from 1978 to 1981, although she never won. In 1980, however, her horse Sonny became the only horse in history to win both the American Quarter Horse Association (AQHA) and the WPRA world championships in the same year.

After being inducted into the Cowgirl Hall of Fame in 1985, Josey continued to compete in barrel-racing events. She went to the NFR again in 1985 and 1987. In 1988, riding Swen Sir Bug, "JC," Josey represented the United States in the Winter Olympics in Calgary, Canada, where she won an Olympic medal. Josey qualified for the NFR in 1989 and again in 1990, on her horse Mr. Revolution Bars, becoming the only cowgirl to go to the NFR in four consecutive decades. Mr. Revolution Bars won the 1990 All American Quarter Horse Congress and was the two-time Wrangler Showdown Champion.

In 1997, Josey rode Orange Smash and won the National Barrel Horse Association Senior World Championship and Reserve Open 1-D Championship

Nine-year-old Mesa Leavitt *(above)* shows off the saddle she won at the twenty-fourth annual Josey Junior Barrel Racers Run for the Roses, held in Marshall, Texas, in May 2005. The event is named for Martha Josey, who began professional barrel racing in 1964, and went to her first NFR in 1968. She returned to the NFR repeatedly over the succeeding years, becoming the only cowgirl to go to the NFR in four consecutive decades.

in Augusta, Georgia. She and Orange Smash went to the NFR again in 1998, winning the third go-round and finishing eighth in the world. In 1999, Josey was chosen as the Women's Sports Foundation-AQHA National Female Equestrian, an annual award. Orange Smash was honored as well, with the 1999 AQHA Best of America's Horse award. Josey and her husband, R. E., a world champion calf roper, now run barrel-racing clinics and produce instructional videos.

CHARMAYNE JAMES

Among barrel-racing fans, there is no greater or more inspirational figure than Charmayne James. According to Wayne Wooden and Gavin Ehringer in *Rodeo in*

Barrel Racing

Charmayne James *(above)* is by far the most successful barrel racer of all time, earning almost $2 million and winning the National Finals Rodeo barrel-racing event eleven times in a row. In 1992, she was inducted into the Cowgirl Hall of Fame.

America: Wranglers, Roughstock, and Paydirt, "Charmayne [James's] . . . legendary status as the queen of barrel racing is forever secure."

In 1984, at age fourteen, riding her horse Scamper, James earned her first NFR championship and set a money-winning record of $53,499 for the year, picking up an additional $20,750 in bonus money as rookie of the year. But that was just the beginning. Over the years, James has earned eleven NFR world championship titles—the most championships in a single event of any rodeo athlete, and the most for any female athlete ever. In 1987, James became the first woman to earn the right to wear the number 1 on her back at the NFR, meaning that she had won more prize money than any other rodeo contestant—male or female—that year. She also holds the record for All Time Leading Money Earner, becoming the first woman to earn $1 million in rodeo prize money in 1990. Her extraordinary success has even landed her in the *Guinness World Records* book.

James retired from rodeo competition in 2002, and currently spends most of her time training horses, conducting barrel-racing clinics on her ranch in Athens, Texas, and conducting traveling clinics around the United States. She has deals with sponsors as varied as a manufacturer of collectable model horses (Breyer International), Coors beer, and Resistol Western hats.

Due in large part to James's unparalleled success in the event, barrel racing has gained a tremendous amount of attention and prestige. James has attracted legions of new fans to the event and inspired many young women to get involved in barrel racing. It will probably be a long time before any of them will be able to beat her accomplishments. Whoever is eventually able to top her will owe her success to the inspiration and trailblazing efforts of Charmayne James.

INTERVIEW WITH CODI WALLACE-BAUCOM, THREE-TIME WORLD CHAMPION BARREL RACER, MAY 16, 2005

Q: How old were you when you started in rodeo?

A: I was in junior rodeos from ages twelve to fifteen, then in regular rodeos from ages nineteen to twenty.

Q: Was barrel racing the first sport you tried?

A: No.

Q: What other rodeo sports have you competed in?

A: Pole bending when I was younger. Now I do breakaway calf roping, too.

Q: Which were your favorite horses to compete with besides Naughty Go Getum, which you rode to the championship this year?

A: He's the main one, but I have a few backup horses. I bought him when he was four, he had won a few futurities, but hadn't done rodeo before. He's eleven now.

Q: What was the worst you ever did in a competition, and why?

A: When Naughty first started doing indoor rodeos he would buck at the second barrel. He still doesn't like indoor shows, he slows down sometimes. I have to keep an eye on him. Not sure why he does it, maybe he can see the crowd more.

Codi Wallace-Baucom *(above)* is an International Professional Rodeo Association (IPRA) world champion barrel racer and was the 2002 IPRA Rookie of the Year. In that same year, her horse, Naughty Go Getum, was the IPRA barrel racing Horse of the Year. She is married to a fellow IPRA competitor, the steer wrestler J. W. Baucom. While competing as a barrel racer, Wallace-Baucom found the time to attend the University of North Carolina and earn her bachelor's degree in exercise and sport science.

Q: Who introduced you to barrel racing and first got you involved in the event?

A: My mom and dad got me into it. My dad used to barrel race, then my mom kind of took it over. They both supported me. Now they're getting older, and my dad's gone back to doing it a little more.

Q: What are you proudest of accomplishing as a barrel racer?

A: My IPRA (International Professional Rodeo Association) rodeo championships. I'm also proud that I'm able to travel to rodeos with my husband and compete. We've been married two years. He's a steer wrestler and a team roper. He motivates me to do what I do. I couldn't do it without him.

Q: Does rodeo or barrel racing run in your family?

A: Just my parents.

Q: Your bio on the IPRA Web site mentioned you'd put your education on hold. Do you plan to go back to school?

A: I think my four-year degree in exercise science and sports is enough. I probably won't go back for my master's.

Q: Do you think that women will move into other rodeo sports eventually?

A: Not really. I think they'll stay where they are. They don't want to get hurt the way you can in some of the men's sports.

Q: And do you think more men will end up competing in barrel racing?

A: There are already a lot! I don't think of it as a women's or men's sport.

Q: What piece of advice would you give someone just starting out that you wish someone had told you?

A: Be confident in your horse. Don't push yourself above the level you're ready for. Go at your own pace.

BARREL-RACING BASICS

CHAPTER 3

A barrel race run according to Women's Professional Rodeo Association (WPRA) rules (which are used by most rodeos locally and nationally) is always run in the same basic way, but the rider may decide whether to start with the right- or left-hand barrel. Barrel races can be run indoors or outdoors in a fenced arena, so long as there is sufficient space.

THE RULES

Here are the basic rules of barrel racing:

1. Three identical barrels are set in a triangular pattern. They must not be weighted or filled with anything, so that if they are tapped by the horse or rider, they will fall over.

2. The rider begins and ends the race at the designated start/finish line. Often there is an electronic-eye device that records the exact moment the horse crosses the line. The rider will race the barrels in a cloverleaf pattern, rounding the two closest barrels (left and right, in either order) first, then the farthest barrel, and then racing straight back to the finish line. If the first turn is done clockwise around the barrel, the next two turns must be counterclockwise, and vice versa, to make a correct cloverleaf pattern *(see diagram on page 19)*.

3. There must be a minimum of 15 feet (4.57 meters) between each of the first two barrels and the side fence; a minimum of 30 feet (9.14 m) between the

third barrel and the back fence; and a minimum of 30 feet (9.14 m) between the start/finish line and the first barrel. There typically will be about 105 feet (32 m) between the nearest barrels (left or right) and the farthest barrel, and 90 feet (27.43 m) between the left- and right-hand barrels, making a slightly uneven triangle.

4. The moment the contestant crosses the starting line, the race's timing will begin, and it will end when horse and rider return across the line after completing their cloverleaf pattern around the barrels.

5. A contestant will be given a "no time" for failing to complete the pattern and a 5-second penalty for knocking over a barrel (in some rodeos, a fallen barrel results in a "no time"). Touching a barrel, including reaching out to keep it from falling over, is permitted without penalty but is a risky maneuver that often results in a fallen barrel.

6. A contestant will be disqualified for running out of turn. It is the contestant's responsibility to know her draw position.

7. A contestant will be given a "no time" if the horse or rider falls during the run in such a manner as to break the pattern, or if the rider falls off the horse.

8. If a barrel is moved off its marker during competition, the barrel must be reset prior to the next competitor's run.

9. Only one horse may be in the arena at any time during competition.

The standard arrangement of barrels, the distances between them, and the pattern horse and rider must follow through the course appear above.

10. Reruns shall be granted if the timer fails to work properly or if the barrels are not placed properly on their markers. No prior penalty will apply to the rerun.

11. The size of the barrel patterns will vary depending on the size of the arena, but the barrel pattern seen in the diagram on page 19 is considered standard.

DRESS CODES

The barrel-racing dress code is a simple one, though it can vary from rodeo to rodeo. In most WPRA events, the contestants must wear:

- A long-sleeved Western shirt

- A cowboy hat (contestants are allowed to wear safety riding helmets instead of cowboy hats if they wish)

- Cowboy boots (most riders choose "ropers," which are flat-heeled)

- Shirt sleeves must be rolled down and buttoned or snapped. Shirttails must be tucked in.

In events sanctioned by the National Barrel Horse Association (NBHA), the world's largest barrel-racing organization, riders who violate similar dress code rules will be fined $25. A rider will also be fined $25 for losing her hat during the NBHA's National, World, and Super shows. For this reason, most riders pin their hats down firmly or use a chin tie to keep it on. Members who don't pay their fines will be ineligible to enter any NBHA shows until they pay up.

Different rodeos may have their own dress codes, but most tend to be similar to that of the NBHA and WPRA. The higher the level or the event, the fancier the outfits tend to be. At championships, riders might deck themselves out in bright shirts with fringe or sequins, with matching colored jeans, fancy boots, and even coordinating protective boots to be worn by their horses. In addition, many riders

A fully decked-out barrel racer and her horse compete in the Mescalero Apache Rodeo, held every year in early July at the Mescalero Apache Reservation in Mescalero, New Mexico. In this photograph, the rider's gear and horse's tack can be clearly identified, including the rider's hat, boots, and Western shirt, and the horse's saddle, saddle blanket, stirrups, reins, bridle, breast collar, and boots.

have superstitions about lucky hats, boots, or other articles of clothing or tokens that they wear or carry on their runs.

EQUIPMENT

In any equestrian sport, a horse needs tack, which refers to the equipment that it wears. This includes a bridle with a bit, reins, saddle, saddle blanket, and, in some cases, additional equipment, such as breast collars that give the saddle additional stability.

In almost all rodeos, Western saddles must be used. The type of bit, or metal bar that a horse wears in its mouth, is up to the rider. There are several different

Barrel Racing

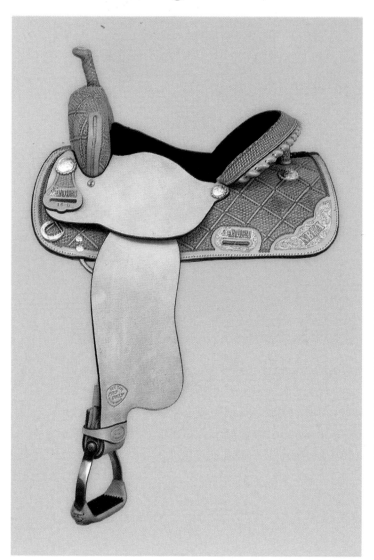

A barrel-racing saddle is pictured at left. Because so much depends upon a horse and rider's speed and maneuverability in barrel racing, barrel-racing saddles tend to be smaller and lighter than most other Western saddles, usually weighing in at less than 30 pounds (13.6 kilograms). The seat tends to be flat, allowing the rider greater ability to maneuver with the horse around barrels. The stirrups tend to be narrow, since it is easier to keep a boot in a narrow stirrup. They are also often covered in rawhide, the toughness of which resists the many scrapes that occur when rubbing up against barrels during a race.

kinds of bits, designed for different riding activities for different kinds of horses. Bits help the rider exert control over the horse, both through steering and slowing up. The bit rests in a natural gap between its front and back teeth. A good rider will always use a light touch on the reins, so that the horse's mouth does not become "hard" or desensitized. Some horses wear boots that cushion and support their muscles and tendons during fast-paced turns. Bell boots are sometimes worn on the hooves so that when running at full speed, the back of the front hooves are not clipped by the back hooves.

THE HORSE

Unlike many other equestrian sports, rodeo events, including barrel racing, do not require riders to use a specific breed of horse, or even to have a pureblood, registered animal. All that matters is the horse's talent, temperament, and ability to learn. Quarter horses are the traditional favorite, because they are considered the fastest and most nimble at short distances and have a calm demeanor. Bréd to have powerful hindquarters that provide them with bursts of speed over a short distance—such as a quarter of a mile (402 m)—quarter horses are favored for many rodeo sports, including cutting, reining, and roping events. But all sorts of horses, from pureblood Arabians to "mutts" of no particular breed, are welcome in rodeo.

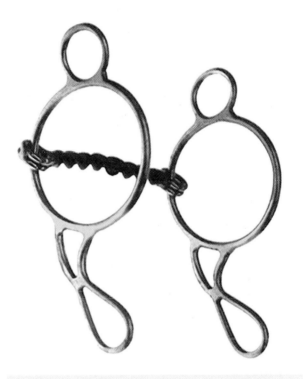

A bit *(above)* is attached to a horse's reins and fits into its mouth. When a rider pulls on the reins, the bit applies pressure, making the horse more responsive to the rider's directions and helping the rider to control the horse's speed and side-to-side motion.

The horse's age and sex are also not a consideration, although stallions (male) are often considered more difficult to handle than mares (female) or geldings (neutered stallions, the most popular among barrel racers). But it's not uncommon to see a seasoned twelve-year-old horse defeat a fiery four-year-old, because barrel racing requires intelligence and maturity as much as it does speed.

Barrel races are now timed using wireless electronic timers rather than stopwatches, helping to eliminate the relative imprecision of the human eye and the lag time that exists in measurements that require hand-eye coordination. A package such as the one pictured above includes two portable wireless electric eyes mounted on tripods. These are set up across from each other at the start/finish line of an arena. An infrared light is beamed between them and timing starts when a horse and rider cross this beam and stops when they cross it again following completion of the course. The time is then provided to the thousandth of a second on the timer console's readout *(center item)*.

TECHNOLOGY AND BARREL RACING

One of the newer developments in barrel racing has been the introduction of cameras and electronic-eye measurements that accurately record a rider's time to a fraction of a second. Previously, barrel racers relied on a judge operating a stopwatch. The accuracy of the times was only as good as the judge's eye-hand coordination and reflexes, as he or she started and stopped the watch based on his or her perceptions of when the horse and rider crossed the start/finish line.

Now, a computer attached to a camera records the horse and rider, and any disputes have to be settled by comparing these records.

RANKINGS

Rodeo champions win based on their performances in their home circuits (rodeos that are held in their geographic region). They then progress to semifinals, national finals, and finally a world championship. Which world championship they enter depends on what associations they belong to, their ability to qualify, and their ability to pay the entrance fees. Barrel racers must "pay to play," much as in horse racing. And, as in horse racing, the purse they win comes partly from those fees. When you see riders' rankings, along with their scores and times will often be a listing of their total winnings in a given year.

At the Wrangler National Finals Rodeo (NFR), the contestant who has won the most money in the previous year earns the right to wear the number 1 while competing. NFR barrel racers make one run a day for ten days. It is physically demanding on both horse and rider, and many racers have backup horses in case their primary horse becomes injured or fatigued.

The barrel racers are ranked based on their aggregate, or combined, score. The scores are based on their times as well as whether they completed the correct pattern and avoided tipping the barrels. The NFR "World Champ" is decided based on ten rounds and the rider's earnings for the year.

THE COMPETITIONS

There are so many barrel-racing organizations that it would be impossible to list all the competitions held each year. Nearly every state has an organization, and there are innumerable 4-H clubs, agricultural fairs, and other local events in which barrel racers compete. The next chapter will discuss these in more detail and explain how to get started in barrel racing.

In the meantime, here is a list of the biggest barrel-racing championships, where the best of the best compete.

Rodeos traditionally begin with an event known as the grand entry. It often features a team of riders who bear rodeo, state, provincial, and national flags, and demonstrate their riding skills and synchronized horse routines. Sometimes the grand entry includes a parade and the singing of national anthems. The grand entry shown above is from the National Finals Rodeo held every year in Las Vegas, Nevada.

Wrangler National Finals Rodeo (NFR)

The Wrangler National Finals Rodeo is the most prestigious rodeo competition in the United States for rodeo athletes. It began in Dallas, Texas, in 1959, and has since moved to Las Vegas, Nevada. The National Finals Rodeo is a PRCA-sanctioned and produced event that lasts for more than a week and features lots of pomp and pageantry—including the Miss Rodeo America beauty pageant. The contestants are narrowed down in a series of competitions, until the final winner of an event is given a gold world championship belt buckle, plus part of a multimillion-dollar purse. The NFR's purse for 2004 was $5.1 million. That year, Molly Powell and her horse took home the gold buckle in barrel racing.

International Professional Rodeo Association (IPRA) World Championship

The IPRA has been awarding world championships to barrel racers since 1961. In 2004, the competition took place in Oklahoma City, Oklahoma. That year's barrel-racing championship was won by Codi Wallace-Baucom of North Carolina, her third championship in a row. In addition to barrel racing, the IPRA Finals Rodeo features bareback bronc riding, bull riding, saddle bronc riding, steer wrestling, and tie-down and team roping.

American Quarter Horse Association (AQHA) Select World Championships

The AQHA holds championships for all kinds of quarter-horse sports, in both youth and adult categories. The 2004 adult champion for barrel racing was Sandi Carver of Prague, Oklahoma, on her mare Tracie's Lucky Lady. The youth champion was Elizabeth Young of Jonesboro, Arkansas, on her gelding Memories to Cherish. The combined purse in 2004 was $2.3 million, which was divided among champions of each class.

National Barrel Horse Association (NBHA) World Championship

Men and women from all over the world came to the United States in 2004 to compete in this championship. There are several different divisions of world champion based on the home district of the riders, including a seniors division for older riders. Purses are more modest in this championship—in 2004, close to $20,000—but other noncash prizes (such as saddles or horse trailers) are awarded as well.

Now that you know the basics and the history of barrel racing, you may be ready to look into becoming a barrel racer yourself. The next chapter will discuss how to get started.

THE RACING LIFE

While barrel racing is a fairly easy sport to understand, there are many tricks of the trade that set apart the merely competent riders from the champions, and that can only be learned through hard work and lots of practice.

Barrel racers begin by competing in local events: rodeos, AQHA-sponsored competitions, or even 4-H events if they are still in grade school or high school. Many barrel racers start racing at a young age—some as young as five years old. Provided a child is old enough to manage her horse or pony, there is most likely a barrel race for her age level. But then again, some barrel racers don't enter their first competition until they're adults. That's the beauty of barrel racing: unlike so many sports, youth doesn't count as much as skill. Quite a few racers continue to compete well into their fifties. As a result, many rodeos have added senior-level competitions. Indeed, as long as you can ride, you can compete.

WHAT YOU NEED

Whatever your age, there are a few basics to getting started in barrel racing. The greatest obstacle to competing is also the most basic and important requirement: a barrel-racing horse. But if owning your own horse is something you can't yet afford or manage, there are still ways to develop your riding skills. Many young people seek out riding instructors who specialize in Western techniques and barrel racing, and who provide a horse to learn on at each lesson.

A handler presents a yearling (a one-year-old horse) to a man interested in purchasing it. Riding and veterinary experts agree that first-time horse buyers should carefully look into the horse's health history, special needs, and habits before purchasing in order to make sure that the horse suits both the buyer's needs and abilities to care for it properly. A first-time buyer and beginning rider should look for a gentle horse that follows guidance.

If you are brand-new to horse riding, it will take a while before you develop solid racing form. If you are a more experienced rider, you will need to take more advanced classes to polish and refine your barrel-racing technique. Besides racing techniques, you will need to learn the basics of reining (also known as Western dressage)—riding with your heels down; sitting properly in the saddle while walking, trotting, cantering, and galloping; holding your reins properly in one hand; and executing various spins, circles, and sliding stops. All of these will help you as a racer, and they will make you look good during the grand entry that begins each rodeo, when the competitors ride around the main arena to show off their horses and their riding technique.

Beginning riders will also need to learn the basics of working with and around horses—how to move so as not to startle them; how to put on and remove all the forms of tack; proper grooming; when, how, and what to feed them; and how to keep them in good health. If you are going to be doing any competing, you are going to need to know how to take the best possible care of your horse at all times. And yes, this will mean that you have to muck the dirty stall! It all comes with the territory.

If you are ready to buy your own horse, do a lot of shopping around and talk to experienced racers about what to look for. You want an animal that is fast and smart, but also teachable and a good fit with your personality. Don't rush into buying the first pretty pony you see. Horses are a major investment. Before you buy, it pays to make sure that you and the horse are a good match, and that it is in good health. Equally important, you must accurately estimate and account for the high cost of boarding the horse, vet bills, food, tack, and travel expenses, including a truck and trailer to transport your horse to competitions. Keep in mind, too, that a horse needs constant riding, bonding, and time spent with its rider outside of competition. A horse's time should not be spent only racing or stalled or it will become bored, depressed, or burnt out. To avoid this, you should take your horse on trail rides and other leisurely riding activities and spend down time bonding and communicating with it.

While you're learning, keep attending rodeos and study the racers carefully in order to pick up tips on technique and equipment choices. Many former champions, such as Charmayne James, offer short clinics for barrel racers. There are many instructional videos available that allow you to learn right at home. There are also instructional, or "how to" books, but barrel racing is difficult to learn by simply studying a diagram on a page. The sport really requires close observation of barrel racers in action and hands-on experience.

GETTING INTO THE GAME

So now you've got your horse, some good tack, lots of practice in the arena, and you're ready to compete! Where do you start?

Beginning riders are often introduced to the speed of barrel racing gradually. In order to begin building a working relationship with the horse and get a good feel for the course's pattern and the motions required, new riders will often approach the barrels first at a walking pace, then a trot, and finally a canter (a faster stride in which all four hooves are off the ground at one point). The above rider approaches a barrel at a walk during a barrel-racing clinic held in Ontario, Canada.

If you know other barrel racers in your area, they're your best resource for what's going on locally. You can go online or to the addresses at the back of this book to get information about organizations like the NBHA and what events they sponsor in your area. If you are in school and you have a 4-H club or Future Farmers of America chapter, they will know where to find local competitions—or they will be sponsoring their own. Use the Internet, pick up the phone, ask around, and you'll most likely find a slew of local competitions that you can enter.

Racers usually join a number of associations during their careers in order to make them eligible for the events that each association sponsors. Memberships almost always come with a fee, however. Coupled with the costs of keeping and caring for a horse, it can get very expensive for a weekend racer who joins several associations. You will have to use your best judgment about how many associations you can afford to join. At the very beginning, you may only have to pay a small entrance fee for local events.

If you're a beginning junior rider, check out your local gymkhanas and junior rodeos. Lots of riders move into the big-time adult rodeos in their early teens, but you might be more comfortable starting out with riders of your own age and skill level. Only you can decide where you need to be competing and when you might move up to the next skill level.

You may start winning right away, or you may not even place for a long time. But if you really love racing the barrels, you should look at each competition as a chance to learn by pitting yourself against your best time. If other barrel racers are faster than you, that just means they have more to teach you!

The National Barrel Horse Association (NBHA), whose logo appears above, is headquartered in Augusta, Georgia, and is the largest barrel-racing organization in the world. The NBHA has more than 23,000 members of all ages and skill levels in the United States, Canada, Italy, France, Panama, and the Netherlands. The association has created various divisions that allow interested barrel racers—whether beginners or experienced professionals, youths or seniors—to compete.

A SPECTATOR'S GUIDE

If you're not really interested in barrel racing yourself, but you love watching and following the sport, then you have it much easier than the competitors! All you have to do is find the time to make it to as many rodeos as possible.

In chapter 3, we explained how barrel racers earn their time. In addition to the sheer speed and skill of horse and rider on display, the drama is heightened when

Barrel racing is an extremely popular sport among young riders, partly because it is a rodeo event in which very young competitors can participate. The NBHA sponsors youth barrel-racing events throughout the United States. Every year it holds the NBHA Youth World Championships for teens (thirteen and older) and youths (twelve and younger). Above, a child competes in a barrel-racing event in Hawaii.

a horse suddenly decides to break its required pattern, or a barrel tips and rocks back and forth, and you don't know whether it's going to fall or not.

In a local rodeo, each rider will usually compete once. In a big national rodeo that occurs over several days, a rider may have to race numerous times, sometimes on different horses. She will be given points toward an aggregate score, as well as compete for other prizes (fastest overall time, most money earned, etc.).

When you're watching a barrel racer, you want to look for how quickly he or she gets off the starting line, how tight their turns around the barrels are, what kind of cloverleaf pattern he or she chooses (beginning left or right), and his or her speed on the final stretch. Because barrel racing is so quick, hitting the first barrel slowly or incorrectly means that the rider will probably not be able to make up much time during the rest of the run. There is very little room for error. In fact, the first barrel is known as the "money barrel." If you don't round it smoothly, cleanly, and quickly, you're probably out of a paycheck.

The nice thing about being a barrel-racing fan is that most barrel racers are approachable and appreciative of their supporters. If they're not too busy, you can usually go up and say hi or congratulate them on a good run when you see them outside the arena or hanging out by the stables. Just remember that you must always ask before touching anyone's horse. You should also never feed someone's horse without first getting the owner's permission. Never ask a barrel racer if you can ride his or her horse. Be respectful of a barrel racer's time. They are very busy with preparations for competition, horse care, and packing up for the next rodeo down the line and have very little free time. If they seem busy, say hi and thank them for their great ride, and then let them get back to work.

CONCLUSION

Every year barrel racing seems to grow a little bigger and draw a little more attention from the sports media. Competitions can now be seen on various sports and local access cable channels, and the Internet has made it easier than ever for fans and competitors to get race results, preview upcoming competitions, and talk to each other about the sport they love.

Part of barrel racing's growing popularity is due to the fact that it is so welcoming to female competitors. Though opportunities for women have opened up in many other sports in recent years, barrel racing still has an appeal few other sports can offer for women who love to ride fast. Barrel racing displays the speed, power, and beauty of a well-trained horse, as well as the unique chemistry forged between horse and rider. Like other rodeo sports such as bull riding or calf roping, barrel racing is as much about skill as risk taking. It's also a sport that's open to all age groups, with a rich history and a proud tradition of giving women a place in the male-dominated world of rodeo. And those who love it will tell you that there's no more exciting moment than when the horse and rider leap out at full tilt toward their first barrel.

Rodeo is a sport with its feet placed firmly in both tradition and spectacle. Originally a way for cowhands to blow off a little steam and show off their roping and riding skills, it has evolved into a million-dollar sport with plenty of glitz and glamor. As rodeo got bigger, sports like barrel racing developed from simple

A male Native American barrel racer approaches and rounds a barrel during a competition at the All Indian Rodeo Cowboys Association (AIRCA) trials held at the Navajo Community College in Tsaile, Arizona, in 1996. AIRCA is a Native American organization that promotes Indian rodeo, chiefly through its sponsorship of the Indian Pro Rodeo Tour. The tour features a series of local rodeos, held mostly in Arizona. Each year, the Indian Pro Rodeo Tour concludes with the National Finals Rodeo, open to Native American rodeo performers who have ridden in at least thirty rodeos that year.

exhibition races into industries with their own champions, celebrities, and legends. Now that barrel racing has spread outside the United States to places as far away as Italy and Panama, its future promises to be as bright and exciting as the event itself.

The National Cowgirl Museum and Hall of Fame in Fort Worth, Texas, has honored the following barrel racers (among other cowgirls):

NAME	YEAR INDUCTED	NAME	YEAR INDUCTED
Elenor "Sissy" Thurman	1975	Shelly Burmeister	1990
Mike Reid Settle	1977	Betty Sims Solt	1990
Rhonda Sedgwick Stearns	1977	Jimmie Gibbs-Munroe	1992
Mary Parks	1979	Charmayne James	1992
Isora DeRacy Young	1979	Marlene Eddleman McRae	
Dora Waldrop	1979		1995
Ann Lewis	1981	Florence Youree	1996
Billie Hinson McBride	1981	Arlene Kensinger	2002
Thena Mae Farr	1985	Velda Tindall Smith	2003
Martha Josey	1985	Sherri Mell	2004

INTERNATIONAL PROFESSIONAL RODEO ASSOCIATION (IPRA) BARREL-RACING WORLD CHAMPIONS

Nancy Finely	1961	Sue Brown	1970
Laura Roberts	1962	Mary Jane Robinson	1971
Laura Roberts	1963	Betty Roper	1972
Mary Cravens	1964	Debbie Keim Robinson	1973
Mary Cravens	1965	Marilyn Kelly	1974
Kerry Grimes	1966	Metha Brorsen	1975
Terry Hearn Blair	1967	Marilyn Duplissey	1976
Terry Hearn Blair	1968	Jyme Beth Powell	1977
Terry Hearn Blair	1969	Jyme Beth Powell	1978

List of Champions

NAME	YEAR	NAME	YEAR
Sherri Dawn Martin	1979	Roxann Dobbins	1992
Sherri Dawn Martin	1980	Jane Melby	1993
Jyme Beth Hammonds	1981	Gayla Channell	1994
Cheri Kraft	1982	Marne Plowman	1995
Sherry Hearn Blair	1983	Betty Roper	1996
Kelli Amos Postrach	1984	Denise Mooney	1997
Sherry Hearn Blair	1985	Betty Roper	1998
Bonnie Russell	1986	Betty Roper	1999
Charla Hartness	1987	Betty Roper	2000
Jeannette Wood	1988	Betty Roper	2001
Connie Lynn Cooper	1989	Codi Wallace-Baucom	2002
Charla Hartness	1990	Codi Wallace-Baucom	2003
Donna Napier	1991	Codi Wallace-Baucom	2004

arena A fenced-in or walled-in area where rodeo events take place. It may be indoors or outdoors and may vary in size.

bronc Short for "bronco"; a horse that has not been fully "broken," or trained to be ridden. In a rodeo, the term refers to horses used in bronc-riding competitions, in which a rider must stay on the horse's back for eight seconds while the horse attempts to buck the rider off.

circuit In a rodeo, refers to the various competitions in which an athlete competes to earn prizes and points that will qualify him or her to compete in larger championship rodeos.

cutting A rodeo sport in which a horse and rider attempt to "cut," or separate, a single cow or calf from a herd within a designated amount of time.

equestrian Someone who rides horses, usually in competitions.

International Professional Rodeo Association (IPRA) One of two national governing bodies for the sport of rodeo, along with the Professional Rodeo Cowboys Association (PRCA). Founded in 1953, the IPRA endorses and sets standards for local rodeos and organizes a world championship, which is held annually in Oklahoma City, Oklahoma. The IPRA has expanded rodeo into international markets, including Canada and Argentina.

National Barrel Horse Association (NBHA) Headquartered in Augusta, Georgia, the NBHA is the largest barrel-racing organization in the world. It has more than 23,000 members of all ages and racing experience across the United States and affiliates in five countries—Canada, Italy, France, Panama, and the Netherlands. NBHA members compete at district, state, national, and world championship levels. The NBHA Youth & Teen World Championships are held the first week of August every year, and the Open & Senior World Championships are held in November.

Professional Rodeo Cowboys Association (PRCA) An association of rodeo athletes created in 1936. The PRCA produces the National Finals

Rodeo, currently one of the most prestigious rodeo championships, and it also runs the Cowboy Hall of Fame.

tack The equipment a rider uses while riding or guiding his or her horse. Generally refers to the bridle, bit, reins, saddle, stirrups, cinches, and blanket, plus other possible equipment such as a halter, lead rope, or neck collar.

Western saddle A type of saddle used in reining (or Western dressage) and rodeo. It is characterized by a pommel, or horn, on the front of the saddle and a raised back edge, as well as stirrups that allow the rider's legs to be nearly fully extended. The saddle evolved to suit the needs of ranch hands—it holds the rider more securely while he or she ropes or herds cattle, and the horn allows riders to loop their ropes around it for better leverage.

Women's Professional Rodeo Association (WPRA) Founded in 1948 as the Girls Rodeo Association (GRA), the group of Texas ranch women began with seventy-four members and sixty approved contests with a total payout of $29,000. Renaming itself the WPRA in 1981, the association now has more than 2,000 members and sanctions about 800 barrel races per year in conjunction with PRCA rodeos, with prize money exceeding $3.9 million. Additionally, its sister organization, the Professional Women's Rodeo Association (PWRA), sanctions all-women rodeo events—including bull riding, bareback, and calf roping—across the United States and holds an annual world championship finals.

For More Information

American Quarter Horse Association
P. O. Box 200
Amarillo, TX 79168
(806) 376-4811
Web site: http://www.aqha.com

International Professional Rodeo Association
2304 Exchange Avenue
Oklahoma City, OK 73108
(405) 235-6540
Web site: http://www.iprarodeo.com/default.htm

National Barrel Horse Association
725 Broad Street
Augusta, GA 30901-1050
(706) 722-7223
Web site: http://www.nbha.com

National Cowgirl Museum and Hall of Fame
1720 Gendy Street
Fort Worth, TX 76107
(817) 336-4475 or (800) 476-FAME (3263)
Web site: http://www.cowgirl.net

Professional Rodeo Cowboys Association
101 ProRodeo Drive
Colorado Springs, CO 80919-2301
(719) 593-8840
Web site: http://prorodeo/org

Women's Professional Rodeo Association
1235 Lake Plaza Drive, Suite 127
Colorado Springs, CO 80906
(719) 576-0900
Web site: http://www.wpra.com

WEB SITES

Due to the changing nature of Internet links, the Rosen Publishing Group, Inc., has developed an online list of Web sites related to the subject of this book. This site is updated regularly. Please use this link to access the list:

www.rosenlinks.com/woro/bara

Brainard, Jack. *Western Training: A Guide to Successful Training, Based on Understanding and Communication.* Colorado Springs, CO: Western Horseman, 2002.

Camarillo, Sharon, Darrell Arnold, and Randy Witte. *Barrel Racing: Completely Revised.* Colorado Springs, CO: Western Horseman, 2001.

Campion, Lynn. *Rodeo: Behind the Scenes at America's Most Exciting Sport.* Guilford, CT: The Lyons Press, 2002.

Hill, Cherry. *Beginning Western Exercises.* Markham, ON, Canada: Storey Publishing, LLC, 1998.

Johnson, Dirk. *Biting the Dust: The Wild Ride and Dark Romance of the Rodeo Cowboy and the American West.* New York, NY: Simon & Schuster, 1994.

Shrake, Richard. *Western Horsemanship: The Complete Guide to Riding the Western Horse.* Colorado Springs, CO: Western Horseman, 2002.

Strickland, Charlene. *The Basics of Western Riding.* Markham, ON, Canada: Storey Publishing, LLC, 1998.

Wright, Ed, Martha Wright, and Glory Ann Kurtz. *Barrel Racing: Training the Wright Way.* Dublin, TX: Equimedia, 1999.

Bibliography

Burt, Don. *The Complete Book of Riding: A Guide to Saddlery, Care and Management, International Breeds, Riding Techniques, and Competition Riding.* New York, NY: Gallery Books, 1989.

Cobb, J. "The Rich History of the National Finals Rodeo." Ezinearticles.com. Retrieved May 3, 2005 (http://ezinearticles.com/?The-Rich-History-of-the-National-Finals-Rodeo&id=27585).

ESPN.com. "Charmayne James: 2002 World Barrel Racing Champion." Retrieved May 3, 2005 (http://sports.espn.go.com/prorodeo/news/story?page=g_stn_James2002Champ).

Hughes, Mary. *Western Riding* (The Horse Library). Philadelphia, PA: Chelsea House Publishers, 2002.

Jordan, Teresa. "Cowgirls." Houghton Mifflin Reader's Companion to U.S. Women's History Online. Retrieved May 2, 2005 (http://college.hmco.com/history/readerscomp/women/html/wh_009000_cowgirls.htm).

Larson, Mary. "UNOHP Rodeo Oral History Project: Pam Minick." Retrieved May 2, 2005 (http://www.unr.edu/cla/oralhist/ohweb/minick.htm).

Mahoney, Sylvia Gann. "Rodeos." *The Handbook of Texas Online.* Retrieved May 1, 2005 (http://www.tsha.utexas.edu/handbook/online/articles/print/RR/llr1.html).

Outrider Books Online. "Bonnie McCarroll's Last Ride." Retrieved May 2005 (http://www.webcom.com/outbooks/1929.html).

Quaid, Ronda. "A Tip of the Hat to the Vaqueros." Santa Barbara News-Press Online, 1996. Retrieved May 3, 2005 (http://www.silcom.com/~imago/sbnp/rodeohist.html).

Saddlezone.com. "The Evolution of the Western Saddle." Retrieved May 3, 2005 (http://saddlezone.com/html-top/saddle_history.htm).

Stanton, Carey. "Island Native Enshrined in Cowgirl Museum." *Galveston County Daily News,* June 9, 2002.

"Try Barrel Racing." WashingtonPost.com, July 25, 2004. Retrieved May 2, 2005 (http://www.washingtonpost.com/wp-dyn/articles/A7504-2004Jul22.html).

Barrel Racing

Wikipedia. "Barrel Racing." Retrieved April 25, 2005 (http://en.wikipedia.org/wiki/Barrel_racing).

Wooden, Wayne S., and Gavin Ehringer. *Rodeo in America: Wranglers, Roughstock, and Paydirt*. Lawrence, KS: University Press of Kansas, 1996.

Worlddressage.com. "History of Dressage." Retrieved May 3, 2005 (http://www.worlddressage.com/history.htm).

WPRA.com. "Women's Rodeo History." Retrieved May 3, 2005 (http://www.wpra.com/rodeohistory.htm).

Index

Barrel Racing

ABOUT THE AUTHOR

Janell Broyles is a native Texan who currently lives in Brooklyn, New York. She spent many happy hours learning Western dressage as a teenager, and still takes every chance she can to go riding. She has written several books for Rosen.

PHOTO CREDITS

Cover, p. 1 © Catherine Karnow/Corbis; p. 4–5 © Kevin R. Morris/Corbis; p. 7 © Swim Ink 2, LLC/Corbis; p. 9 postcard courtesy of Bob Bovee; p. 11 National Cowgirl Museum and Hall of Fame, Fort Worth, Texas; p. 13 © AP/Wide World Photos; pp. 14, 16 photos by Walter Smith; p. 21 © Dave G. Houser/Corbis; pp. 22, 23 photos courtesy of Tex Tan, Yoakum, Texas; p. 24 photo courtesy of R. U. Ready Electronics Ltd; p. 26 photo by John Gurzinski; p. 30 © Richard Smith/Corbis; p. 32 courtesy of Highland Wilderness Tours; p. 33 courtesy of the National Barrel Horse Association; p. 34 © Richard A. Cooke/Corbis; p. 37 © Kevin Flemming/Corbis.

Designer: Les Kanturek